Remembering to Breathe

5 Easy Exercises for Caregivers to Reclaim a Healthy Work-Life Balance

Melissa Valdellon, O.D.

IMPORTANT MEDICAL DISCLAIMER: This book is intended as a reference volume only, and not as a medical manual. The information given here is designed to help you make informed decisions about your health. It is not intended or implied to be a substitute for any treatment prescribed by, or medical advice given by, your doctor. All of the content, including text, images, and information contained in this book is for general purposes only. If you suspect that you have a medical problem or have any concerns whatsoever, please seek competent medical help immediately.

REMEMBERING TO BREATHE. Copyright © 2015 by Melissa Valdellon. All rights reserved. This book may not be reproduced in whole or in part, stored in a retrieval system, or transmitted in any form or by any means – electronic, mechanical, or other – without written permission from the copyright holder, except by a reviewer, who may quote brief passages in a review.

Published by Melissa Valdellon
www.melissavaldellon.com

Editing by Stephanie Gunning
Cover design by kelvintang
Author photograph by Jennifer Michelson

ISBN-13: 978-0692402924
ISBN-10: 0692402926

DEDICATION

To all the caregivers out there, like my mom and dad, who give, and give, and give, without thought of getting anything back. This is for you.

CONTENTS

	Introduction	i
1	Defining Stress	1
2	The Benefits of Stress Management Exercise 1	5
3	Acknowledging and Processing Stress Exercise 2	8
4	Finding Your Calm When You're Under Pressure Exercise 3	14
5	The Schedule, Keeping It Real Exercise 4	17
6	Gratitude Exercise 5	22
7	Laughter Bonus Exercise	25
	What's Next?	27
	About the Author	29

INTRODUCTION

In today's world, finding a calm moment for yourself amidst all that you do to take care of your patients and loved ones is getting to be harder and harder. When was the last time you went five minutes without attempting to finish a task from a long to-do list of things that needed to be done yesterday – all while also trying to give 100 percent of your attention to someone you're helping at the moment? All the incessant distractions, like hearing a phone ring, having a chattering coworker interrupt you, and seeing multiple text notifications pop up on your cell phone are probably not helping you remain calm either, right? Thankfully, there are ways to address the need to reclaim your balance that are easy to implement.

The exercises in *Remembering to Breathe* are designed to address your specific stress triggers and help you work through them. Written in a concise and accessible manner, this book is especially intended for caregivers – both professional and personal – who suffer from stress and burnout as they ceaselessly give of themselves to patients, friends, and family. As a lifetime student learning how to cultivate a balanced mind-body-spirit connection myself, I've read countless books and articles on the subject of stress management, meditation, and holistic self-care, and I've also tested many types of exercises to see what truly works in achieving a balance between mind, body, and spirit. Health care providers, family caregivers, students, and many others who struggle with work-life balance have already experienced great success by implementing the exercises found in this helpful how-to guide.

I promise that by the end of this book, you'll have learned about different kinds of stresses and stress triggers and how stress affects the mind and body. You'll also have picked up some useful tips and techniques to help you manage the pressure in your life and overcome your stress.

1

DEFINING STRESS

Dear Caregiver:

You regularly take care of and help some very important people: your partner, your children, your parents, and your patients or clients. You were probably raised to take care of others and place their needs before your own. But have you ever taken the opportunity to care for the needs of the most important person in your life?

I hope you know that I'm referring to you.

The demands of caring for others take a great deal of our personal time and effort, and at the end of the day, often too little energy remains to put even a little bit of attention on our own needs. It doesn't help that in modern society, we find ourselves constantly bombarded by high expectations to do and be everything for our family, our coworkers, and our colleagues. We've been taught to say yes to every request and raised to believe that the very idea of saying no is selfish and perhaps even disrespectful. Even more problematic, caregivers often suffer from guilt or feelings of inadequacy when they think to seek help for themselves. This is a society that expects us to be at the top of our game, giving it our all, 100 percent of the time. In other words, we are called to be a "perfect" Superman or Superwoman.

These external pressures are confounded by internal stressors like fear, uncertainty, and worry. How often have "what ifs" concerning the past or future left you sleepless at night? It's like we want to continue haunting ourselves, replaying things we said or did that we wish we could take back, or imagining how future events outside of our control will play out in a myriad of usually disastrous ways. Then we also play a constant comparison game, taking stock of what we have in our lives and seeing if we're better or worse off than the neighbors across the street. That leads, in turn, to another round of trying to figure out how to achieve the next goal – the better car, the better house, the latest in technology. Truthfully, it's no wonder we find ourselves overwhelmed and maybe wondering if there's a point to any of it in the end.

Right now, an online search on stress management yields list after list of tips on how to cope with stress. Such tips include learning to say no, avoiding people or situations that cause stress, managing your time better, shifting to a more positive mindset, relaxing, making time for yourself, and adopting a healthy lifestyle. Truly, there are a lot of helpful resources out there that teach different ways to manage stress, and you've probably gone through many of the exercises those resources offer already with some success.

But what many of these lists neglect to address is the connection between the mind, body, and spirit, which altogether defines our overall health and well-being. That's why it's so hard sometimes, despite our best efforts, to follow the suggestions and guidelines outlined for us by a doctor, counselor, or other reputable source, to maintain a stress-free mindset.

The stress response is a biological process. The body naturally wants to maintain a level of internal stability and balance, or homeostasis. The body breaks down what it takes in, into useful parts it needs and efficiently discards the rest. When the body encounters a condition that disturbs or shifts its equilibrium, the body then mounts a stress response in an attempt to realign itself to its normal condition or function by reducing or eliminating the original stressor or threat.

Physiologically, stress hormones are released in response to any type of threat. These chemicals act on various parts of the body, causing an increased heart rate; quick, shallow breathing; dilated eyes; a temporarily decreased response to pain sensations; and more. All this is done to help us increase our focus and reaction time in making the snap assessment of whether this is an appropriate time to stay and fight or to flee the situation. This fight-or-flight response has served our species biologically in the past when we were being confronted by, say, a bear in nature, but it doesn't serve the same purpose when we are stuck in, for instance, another afternoon's rush hour traffic.

So going back to the idea that stress is a natural response to imbalance, you can see that stress itself cannot be labeled as entirely good or bad. Short, acute bouts of stress are natural and can actually be of benefit to us, as in the adrenaline rush we may feel during the last few minutes we spend tidying up a presentation before a deadline. What stresses one person versus another is highly subjective. Some of us are easily stressed and others are unflappable.

If the stress hormones circulating in our bloodstreams accumulate over time, however, they start taking a toll on our physical bodies. Chronic stress creates physical, emotional, and mental changes that ultimately can lead to high blood pressure, heart disease, heart attacks, diabetes, headaches, gastrointestinal problems, anxiety, depression, and even cancer. The body is more prone to sickness with a weakened immune system since stress weakens our immunity.

Long term stress can lead to behavioral changes in sleep patterns, diet, and even an increase in addictions as a way of coping. On a larger scale, any of these changes can affect external relationships. We may find ourselves resentfully snapping at the very people we care about most, or we may find our productivity slipping at work. Any and all of this can affect our self-esteem, which leads to more stress, thus perpetuating the downward spiral toward burnout.

Everyone experiences stress and responds to it in his or her own way, as we all have different tolerance levels in response to different stressors. I know plenty of my colleagues have been able to push through a daily routine of caring for patients all day long, for ten or twenty years, with no obvious signs of distress. They likely have highly effective coping mechanisms that work for them. Put another individual in their shoes though, and that person might find himself or herself at a breaking point after only a month or a week into the experience. Part of managing stress, then, is deciding how to react in a given situation and manage one's thoughts and feelings. This ability varies from individual to individual. With practice, we all can learn to do better at coping with our stress triggers.

In any case, let's begin to uncover exactly why managing stress is important in the next chapter.

2

THE BENEFITS OF STRESS MANAGEMENT

In today's competitive, technologically savvy world, effective stress management is necessary to successfully maintain a healthy work-life balance. We have already seen how constant negativity can snowball into something beyond our control. Too much stress can build and take a physical and mental toll on us. Thankfully, reducing stress and maintaining a positive outlook can create a healthy ripple effect that grows into something bigger than you expected, too.

First off, less stress means that excess fight-or-flight hormones go back to normal levels and stop wreaking havoc on the body. When you achieve a natural balance point physiologically, all the health problems listed previously, such as high blood pressure, fluctuating blood sugar levels (as in diabetes), and bodily pains diminish. It is important at this point to continue discussions with your physician to see if medications can be adjusted at this point – NOT before. With an improvement to health, you may find yourself with an improved sleeping schedule, more dedication to eating a healthy diet, and more energy to take up exercise and other activities again.

More energy translates directly into an increase in productivity in the workplace, as daily tasks are more easily accomplished when we're calm and centered. In the long run, this means that the people you give care to, or whose needs you're providing for, are getting your undivided attention, as well as the high quality of care that you want to give and that they are seeking. You not only regain a sense of accomplishment and pride in your work when you perform well, but your relaxed demeanor also fosters a warm and trusting relationship between you and your patients.

The positive ripple effect continues in your personal life when you bring the same sense of trust and warmth to close relationships. You may find that it's easier to spend quality time with family and loved ones, making your relationships more fulfilling after, and even during, periods of stress.

With each accomplishment you make at work or at home, the negative thoughts, the self-doubt, and all the stressed mental chatter shift more and more toward positive themes and thoughts promoting self-care.

And it all starts with a single action, or a single thought. Even the simple act of reading this book points to the fact that you're taking an active step towards taking care of yourself. With time and practice, you'll gain confidence and come to know that you can overcome even the biggest levels of stress.

So that being said, let's jump into our first exercise. It's a simple one.

Exercise 1: Set and Declare Your Intent

An intention is more than just the act of setting a goal. It involves adding your energy, focus, and spirit to your desired outcome. So what do you want after reading this book? Or what do you want in relation to your stress?

Your intention can be simply to be less stressed. It can be being more open to allowing loved ones to help. It can be to learn how to take more active steps in reducing stress in your life.

I find it helpful to do this quick exercise each morning when I first wake. Before allowing the list of tasks I want to get accomplished that day to start forming in my head, I lay still for a moment of peace and give gratitude for waking up to another beautiful day. Then I state my intent for that day, something along the lines of: Let me be guided to do all that I am meant to do, to reach out and help all whom I am meant to touch, and to be open to all the miracles manifesting before me all day long.

I often repeat the exercise at night, stating the intention of getting a solid, good night's rest so that I can start a new day again with renewed energy.

For me, I purposely leave the intentions wide open, allowing for the best, and even better, things to come my way. This sets the tone I want for the day. If I intend that only A, B, and C are going to happen (for example, I finish that report for work, I get the kids to soccer practice on time, and my partner and I go to bed without another argument over the bills), that doesn't leave as much wiggle room for other surprises to come my way that may actually even be better for me in the long run.

Take a moment now to state your present intent. You can do it out loud, silently in your head, or put it to pen and paper. Set it right now and then repeat the process as often as you need to, such as before a big presentation, to remind yourself of what you want.

Make this intention-setting time a sacred time for the next couple of minutes. It doesn't have to be long, and again, an intention doesn't have to be very specific. Just hold the intention with love and openness, and watch the miracles unfold.

Does your spirit feel better yet?

I hope you can see how reducing stress will have huge implications for you, as a caregiver, at the physical, mental, soulful, and interpersonal levels – and likely even beyond, as happiness and positivity rub off on the people you interact with. People you work with, people you care for, and even the people you pass on the street, may feel the effects of your reduction in stress and benefit from feeling more relaxed and happy, too.

3

ACKNOWLEDGING AND PROCESSING STRESS

It has been said that the first step to solving a problem is to acknowledge it. Communicating the real reasons for your stress to your family, friends, and even doctors and counselors is a very important step that should not be neglected. They can all be a wonderful support system, a built-in source of help and relief, if you let them.

As we've seen, when stress is left to build and build without any outlet or relief, it becomes overwhelming, and its negative effects can affect others in our lives. Ideally, we want to manage stress and neutralize its effects before it evolves into something more and creates any symptoms or diseases. So let's go into our second exercise with the idea that you've already received assistance and support from others, but are now seeking something more. This exercise is going to have you go inward. Change cannot occur unless you yourself want it enough and take the first step. Trust me, you aren't alone in your stress. I'll guide you through this.

Exercise 2: Release Your Stress

First, take out a piece of paper and your preferred writing utensil — a pen, a pencil, a crayon, a marker, whatever. If you prefer, you can instead create a new document on your computer. Using a voice recorder is yet another option if you have the technology. The goal of this exercise is to use some kind of physical medium to receive your thoughts.

Next, set a timer for ten minutes and let everyone know that you won't be available during that interval. That means turning your phone on silent and putting it away, turning off any notifications on your computer, and putting a sign on the door and shutting it. If needed, go walk your dog real quick and give a treat to keep him or her quietly busy for the next few minutes. You may wish to wait until the rest of the household is asleep or schedule this during part of your lunch break. Do whatever it takes. Do not let yourself be disturbed for the next ten minutes. You've already taken one step towards healing your stress by purchasing this book. Keep up the trend of self-care by giving yourself ten minutes.

When you're ready, settle comfortably into your seat. Once you press start on your timer, write out, doodle out, type out, or speak out your thoughts and impressions about anything and everything that is giving you stress. Do NOT just do this in your head. The point of this exercise is to get your mind and body to work together in releasing the stress. Go ahead. Get it all out and be specific.

Talk about how weighed down you feel when you give, and give, but get little to no support in return.

Write out your frustrations about how your patient, your spouse, or your child didn't listen to you the first five times you asked for them to do something.

Spill the beans on how you were so tired this morning when you woke up because you couldn't get to sleep until after midnight. You were tossing and turning as thoughts of what you need to do in the morning kept you up.

Draw out the anxiety you feel from knowing that you're going to be giving a speech at a family reunion or company gathering next week, and that you're afraid of making a fool of yourself on stage – and that the audience will never let you live it down afterward.

Think of all the ways that a worst-case scenario could take place, and write down those "what ifs." I find that when I come to writing about these "what if" statements, I try to put the situations in perspective: Am I going to die? Will this cause death to someone else? Unless you're a caregiver dealing directly with life-or-death situations, death is an unlikely (although still valid) concern, so write what you have to say in regard to those "what if" situations.

Now, from the examples above, I hope it's obvious that it doesn't matter how big or how small you believe your frustrations are, or whether the stressors come from external or internal sources. Get it out! Whatever it is, it's bothering you. It's stressing you out and you need to release this before it builds into something bigger. The best thing to do is to start letting it out with this safe and private exercise that you don't have to share with anyone.

And if you think you've written enough or spoken enough and the ten minutes aren't up – keep going! Keep writing, keep typing, keep speaking, even if it's just to acknowledge that you're stressed by doing the exercise and the fact that you have no idea if it's going to help you out. Keep going.

No one is here to judge you or what you're going through. You've needed this release on so many levels and I applaud you for going through this exercise. No one needs to know the specifics except you. Just keep going. Ten minutes. No less.

Of course, if the ten minutes fly by and you feel like you've just barely started describing everything that's on your mind and in your heart, by all means, keep going until you feel that you're truly, truly complete. That's it. When you're ready, I'll catch you in the next section.

Take a deep breath and shake off all of the stressful feelings you brought up in doing the exercise. Give your hand a chance to recover from clenching your pen. Roll your shoulders a few times and rock your head back and forth. Clear your throat and drink some water.

How are you feeling?

I know that this exercise can be pretty intense, but hopefully you are feeling lighter now that you've let some stress out. With any luck, you are noticing that you can breathe easier, that there's less tension overall in your body.

Or perhaps you feel sadder because you feel like a failure in not being able to deal with all that stress better. Or maybe you're more angry and frustrated than ever before.

Whatever you are feeling is okay and normal.

Take a moment now to take three deep breaths. As you breathe, know and acknowledge the fact that you are human and have your own unique set of trials and obstacles to overcome – along with the famous actor on screen, the spiritual leader, and the beggar on the street corner. We are all humanly perfect in our own way already, with our triumphs, faults, stresses, and all.

As I mentioned to someone recently, how you deal with a person or a situation helps define who you are. We are each challenged daily with multiple situations that could give us stress. Think back on how you typically respond to a new challenge, whether it is anticipated or comes seemingly from nowhere. Do you normally let stress wash over you without a second thought? Or does the stress eat at you and keep you up at night (in which case, I suggest doing the first exercise over again if you're feeling incomplete or catch another wave of stress-related thoughts and emotions)?

Or, more likely, you've noticed that your reaction tends toward one or the other, and it depends on the situation.

We'll talk about shifting mindsets later on in this book. For now, just take a moment to process what happened when you did the first exercise. Essentially, you performed a massive brain dump, taking the first step to relieve yourself of all the mental baggage you've been carrying.

Now what do you do? The next step is for you to let it go.

If you wrote a list of stressors on a piece of paper, rip the list into smaller and smaller pieces. You could also just put the whole sheet through a shredder and dump the scraps straight out into your recycling bin. If you're so inclined, burn the paper. A candle or other small, contained flame will do.

If you happened to magically have done this exercise on dissolvable paper (who knew such a thing existed?), give the paper to water. Watch as the words and paper disappear.

If you completed this task on a computer, the letting go process is even easier. Simply don't save the file. Close the program. If you already saved it, delete it now.

Do the same thing if you recorded your thoughts vocally. Delete the audio.

What do you have to gain by keeping the burden of stress with you? Is it truly serving you and helping you accomplish what you want or need to do? This may be the case for people who use stress as a motivational force and inspiration towards activity. More often though, it can be distracting and reach unhealthy levels when not properly addressed.

The point of this exercise then is to physically, mentally, and also symbolically let go of the stress that is weighing you down. Imagine that all of the stress, frustration, anger, sadness, and heavy feelings you've identified are just disappearing and vanishing into thin air.

If you're so inclined, feel free to ask God, or an angel, or a spirit guide that you're close to, or whatever helps you, to help take the stress away for you. Once you're done, know that the burden is no longer yours to manage, that it will all be taken care of as needed.

Whatever you need to do, just let it go (cue super catchy music here). Understand that worrying about the stress isn't itself changing the reality of the situation. Acknowledge it as a tool to help you achieve something better. This is heavy work we're doing, so please be gentle with yourself as you go through this process.

You may find yourself needing to repeat the first exercise multiple times to get through everything, or repeating the exercise anytime something new happens in your life that causes you to be moved off balance.

You may have been carrying the same stress and weight around for a long time – maybe even for years or decades. Remind yourself that you are supported and loved. Take the time to acknowledge the big step you're taking and then let the stress go.

I'll see you in the next chapter.

4

FINDING YOUR CALM WHEN YOU'RE UNDER PRESSURE

Let's say that you look at the next patient on your schedule or glance into the waiting room and see that the patient you've been dreading seeing this entire shift is next. This individual always comes with a list of complaints a mile long and wants you to listen intently as he goes through every single ailment and treatment he's tried in detail. While you want to do your best to attend to his needs, you can't help but feel uncomfortable and anxious anytime you see him.

Or let's say that you're in the middle of preparing for a gathering, like your child's first birthday party, and while you're still setting the table, you see a parent and child arrive who hadn't confirmed that they would be attending, and there's actually no room for them to sit.

What goes on for you when you're thrown into a situation that either you have anticipated and are facing with dread, or have had no way of preparing for ahead of time? Physiologically, the stress response may be initiated that takes you into fight-or-flight mode. Hopefully, there's no fighting at the children's birthday party or in your office. And hopefully you can do better than running away.

Mentally, I can only imagine the choice words that could be going through your mind as it scrambles to find an acceptable solution to the situation besides fleeing or fighting.

What I invite you to do in the moment instead is to breathe.

Exercise 3: Breathe

The breath has a way of grounding and centering the mind and allowing it to regain perspective. It activates the relaxation response, which keeps the body from releasing a tidal wave of stress hormones that affect our judgment and are likely not helpful in a challenging situation.

This exercise doesn't have to take long. It takes a few seconds, maximum. But the few seconds you do take can make a huge difference.

Use this exercise anytime you start feeling like your stress is building up to something out of your control and you need a moment to collect yourself.

To start the exercise, stop moving and then remain still. If you need to sit in a chair, do so. If you are standing and feel like you can continue in that position, that's fine, too.

Close your eyes and just take a slow, deep breath. See how long it takes to breathe in and then slowly exhale. Mentally, place all your focus on the physical act of the breath for those few seconds. Repeat this focused breath a couple more times. Once you've done this and you're ready, you can open your eyes and continue on.

If you have a little bit more time to go deeper with this exercise, I want you to take notice of the support under your feet if you're standing, or the chair you're sitting on if you're seated. Is the seat firm or soft, with cushions? Is your back straight, or are you slumped over in a more comfortable position? Do you have your legs crossed? Are your feet able to touch the floor?

There is no right answer here. Just notice and see how much more comfortable you can make yourself.

Once you're ready, I want you to take your left hand and place it lightly on your chest. Breathe in, and feel your chest lift and expand. As you exhale, feel your chest come back down.

Now take your right hand and place it lightly on your belly. Do the same thing. Breathe in and see if you can get the air to puff out your stomach area. Does it contract when you breathe out?

As you continue breathing, notice where your body is moving.

With each breath, keep your focus on your chest and stomach area. Be aware of the natural process of breathing and don't try to push yourself to feel anything else right now. All that's important in this moment is your breath. Notice as it goes in . . . and as it flows out.

Continue this process for the next couple of minutes. Aim for five. If you can do it, great! See if you can keep going! If not, no need to bring judgment in. This is simply an exercise to bring you back to your breath.

Do the breathing exercise as many times as you need throughout the day or week. Anytime you feel stressed and need to take a moment to yourself, take a moment or two to close your eyes, go inward, and just breathe. I promise that after those one or two minutes, or even the few seconds you can spare for one long, slow breath, your mind will have regained some clarity about the situation at hand and you'll be more focused when you finally do open your eyes.

5

THE SCHEDULE, KEEPING IT REAL

Stress prevention is key to self-care. We've already discussed how when we're busy taking care of other people, we often forget to take care of ourselves. When we get caught up with the bills to pay, laundry to do, food to cook or pick up, and a home to maintain, on top of the full list of things we need to do at work, it's easy to feel lost and overwhelmed.

A component to successful stress prevention includes shifting your perception away from one of victimhood. To do so is not easy, but rather than wondering, "Why did this happen to me?" or focusing on a thought such as "everyone else around me is doing so much better," try shifting your negative beliefs toward something more empowering. Take charge of your stress levels by changing what is in your power to change, especially if you see a pattern to your stress.

Taking charge also means actively limiting the sources of stress in your life. This may mean making the decision to leave a job or a partner. It could mean not engaging in the gossip at work or watching the news right before bed.

Maintaining low stress with self-care helps keep stress at more manageable levels. This includes prioritizing activities that you find fulfilling, be it listening to music, exercising, or reading inspirational literature. Make it a point to do at least one thing you love daily and watch your stress melt away, even if it's just for a few moments.

Now, all of this talk on taking time for oneself is nice, but that still doesn't address how you will get everything on the to-do list done. Let's turn our attention to that now.

Exercise 4: Organize Your Schedule

One thing you can do is to create a checklist. This to-do list is different from the intention list we covered previously.

Speaking for myself, I set my intentions before I leave bed and then purposefully hold off on formulating my checklist for the day until after I eat breakfast and have gained the clarity and energy I need. Once my head is in the right "space," I can make my list of the day's tasks in the brain dump fashion we attempted earlier with our stress lists, thereby decluttering the mind space from these tasks.

Now, there are a lot of different ways to write out your list. Most common is the tried-and-true checklist method on paper. I find this usually doesn't work for me because it isn't specific or flexible enough when I attempt one. I can't sort by priority or move items around to another date if something comes up. And I find that keeping a continuous list of items that gets added to and subtracted from daily is just too messy for me, even if I start with a fresh list each day.

For a while, I followed the four quadrant to-do list method that differentiated tasks by levels of importance and due date (see image below).

	Due Soon	Not Due Soon
Important		
Not Important		

This method was great when I was able to have a physical representation of the grid on a white board. It allowed me to be flexible, move items around, and visually prioritize them. However, I found that in shifting to a more digital lifestyle and no longer having the grid always present in my field of view, I was unable to digitally replicate it easily, and therefore greatly reduced my reliance on it.

Recently, I've taken to placing tasks directly into my online calendar, which I know I will consult at least a few times daily. I include the daily things, like going to the dog park or getting groceries. I also put in planned phone calls with colleagues and clients. I've always put conferences and vacations in my schedule, but now I've started to put the planning steps in my online calendar also.

For example, I'm planning on taking a trip to New Orleans in a few months for a major conference. I placed the dates of the conference in my calendar long ago and also the opening registration date. Recently, I marked a date in my calendar to start looking at hotels in the area, I made a deadline to book airline tickets, and I chose a date to give myself an hour to look up the restaurants I want to eat at while I'm in the area. I've also set reminders to start putting money away to help pay for the trip.

By spreading all those planning items out over the course of the next few months, I don't have to stress out about them before the conference registration has officially opened, or stress out when I realize the conference is only a month away and I haven't formally planned for anything yet. By committing to spreading out the planning process ahead of time, I know I've released a lot of the potential stress I could feel over the things that need to be done leading up to the conference.

For another example, let's say you've received an invitation to a friend's wedding a few months down the line. You could break down your planning the same way I did with my conference. Put down the date and look at what else is going on in your life around that time. Is there a big project going on at work that you're already involved in? By identifying potential time conflicts, you can anticipate that you'll have to work harder in the weeks and months ahead to get the bulk of things done before you head off to celebrate with your friend. Put dates down that you'll need to reserve time in your schedule on which to book flights and a hotel room, buy a new outfit for the event, purchase a wedding gift, and so forth. In this way, it doesn't all have to happen at once and you won't get stressed about it.

What about a big task, like cleaning out a garage? The thought of spending a day, or even half a day, on a task like this can be pretty daunting. My suggestion is to break that task up into smaller units. Dedicate forty-five minutes every week or month to getting the task done. Three-quarters of an hour doesn't sound like much, but you'd be surprised at how much can be accomplished when you're focused solely on the task at hand. Over time, progress builds and you may even find yourself resetting the timer once you're in the swing of things so you can keep going on a particular day. Take the time to declutter the garage or anywhere else in your house that needs attention. Doing so frees up space and gives you motivation to tackle other tasks down the road when see what you've accomplished.

I usually don't block general tasks into a certain hour of the day. For me, the commitment is in writing it down and knowing I will spend 30-60 minutes on the task, depending on the complexity. For example, today, I need to look for a new vet. Tomorrow, I'm going through the closet to find things to donate. The day after, I'm going to continue working on a case report for submission a couple months down the road. I know these tasks will vary in length, but looking at the calendar reminds me of what I want to accomplish that day, knowing that some tasks have future dates building on those accomplishments. If my other commitments end up taking more time than I've anticipated, I'm free to move a planned task to another free day where there is a 30-minute gap.

Now I'm not saying that this is the only way to tackle your to-do list, or that every single minute of the day needs to be accounted for. Whatever works for you in terms of your daily or weekly or monthly list is great! No need to change a thing unless you want to try something new to see if works even better than your current habits. If you have another way of being productive that doesn't involve lists, please share it with me! The point is to make sure to consult your calendar periodically to ensure you're on task.

Getting your to-do list out of your head and down on paper helps to declutter the mind of extra stress in terms of knowing exactly what needs to be done, and by when. Breaking big tasks into smaller, more manageable parts means reducing stress, too, by avoiding last-minute preparations to get things done. By knowing what's exactly on your plate and when, you can give it more focus and be more conscious of what you're doing at any given time.

And who knows? By doing this, you may even find yourself having more free time to do other things, like exercise, plan a fun date with a loved one, or catch up on episode or two of your favorite show. The choice is yours.

One more thing about the schedule: Think long and hard about immediately saying yes to every request that comes your way. If anything else, ask for a couple moments to glance at your schedule. Keep your calendar handy so you can readily check before committing yourself to take on that extra project at work, the extra baking duties for school, the party coming up this weekend, and so on.

Ask yourself: Are you saying yes because you can readily and easily commit? Or are you saying yes because it's expected of you? Does saying yes mean you can save face now and come up with an excuse to back out later when you actually think about it? Can the task be delegated to someone else or re-scheduled to a more opportune time? Remember, you've committed to decreasing stress in your life. Sometimes, that means saying no and putting your needs first for the time-being.

6

GRATITUDE

We've covered a lot of ground already. We've defined what stress is and how it has played a role in your life, practiced how to release current stress, practiced an exercise to take you out of immediate stress by breathing, gone over how to prevent stress from occurring, and explored ways to promote self-care.

That is certainly a call for celebration!

For you, a caregiver who has given of yourself time and time again to the people you love and to the people you work with and work for, I give my sincerest congratulations on taking these very important steps to start regaining balance in your life. Even more importantly, I am so grateful that you are now giving yourself the care you deserve.

This leads us to our last exercise, which truly helps in creating a strong link between the mind, body, and spirit. It is an exercise for making gratitude a deep-rooted practice in your conscious mind. As important as it is to say please and thank you, I truly believe that giving gratitude should be just as ingrained in our thoughts.

Exercise 5: Live in Gratitude

At the end of each day, I make it my habit to list at least three things I'm grateful for. These could be events that occurred that day, or items that I'm generally happy for. By mentally recalling events over the course of the day, physically writing these events in a journal, and experiencing gratitude as I relive the moments, it becomes much easier to achieve a state of awareness and balance.

Since I started doing this practice, my journal has become full of mentions of things that continue to inspire and comfort me, especially in times of stress. Some items, I repeat again and again. For example, I am grateful:

- For the warm cuddles I get from my pets.
- For being able to witness a beautiful sunset or sunrise today.
- For having shelter, food, and a comfortable bed to sleep on.
- For the people in my life.

Some items are specific for a given day. For example, I am grateful:

- For the hug I got from my grandmother patient today.
- That my nephew decided to read quietly with me after dinner, rather than ask to play with his loud train set.
- That the car worked perfectly for me today after it gave me problems the last couple of mornings.
- That I was able to read another chapter of the book I've been working on for a couple months.

Take a child who automatically says thanks to an aunt for a not-so-great gift only when prompted, as opposed to the child who gets the dream toy he's wanted and waited for (and perhaps even worked hard for), and finally receives it. Words of gratitude don't even need to be said in that moment, but you can be sure that he is feeling an enormous amount of genuine gratitude as he screams in delight and jumps up and down with excitement. That pure joy is the emotion I want you to try and capture each time you do this exercise.

By knowing that I have to write at least three things down each night, I have found that I'm more mindful during the day, watching for things that I appreciate and love rather than focusing on the things that go wrong. Again, it may take time for this shift to occur in your mind, but I can definitely say that looking for the good in life is not a bad habit to create.

Be grateful for the big and the small things in your life. It may feel weird at first, but expressing gratitude is another tool for keeping things in perspective. What is ten minutes of not being able to find your keys worth compared to being able to share a meal with loved ones? What is the pain of being stuck in traffic for an extra fifteen minutes compared to the kiss from your child or partner when you get home? Which are you going to remember and treasure in the end?

I am grateful that you have picked up this book today. I am grateful that you have stuck with me this far. Most importantly, I'm grateful you're making the attempt to take care of you.

7

LAUGHTER

In this book, I've attempted to highlight how stress brings about changes physically, mentally, and soulfully. Remember that these three aspects of our being are interconnected. Therefore, it's important to take care of the body through proper diet and exercise, use medications as directed by your physician, and shift your mindset from one focused on stress to one focused on clarity and creating outcomes. Doing these will help as you strive to regain the healthy work-life balance you sought when you first picked up this book.

I wanted to highlight for a moment a couple of ways to take care of the spirit and make our discussion complete.

Whatever your beliefs, if you have a faith in a specific religion or ideology, or even if you do not, I honor that in you. My sincerest hope, though, is that you have found something worth believing in and that you can draw strength from it, be it God, the Universe, Source, or whatever you call it. Maybe you draw strength from the smile on a loved one's face. Or maybe from knowing there will be another day tomorrow, when you can try to do your best all over again. That's worth something.

To help boost the spirit then, my parting thought is to keep the faith and to keep it light.

Bonus Exercise: Laugh

The last exercise I want you to practice is laughter. Besides gratitude, joy and humor have a way of lifting up the spirits that nothing else can.

So I give you permission right now to laugh so hard that your belly shakes. Seriously, laugh as hard as you can – even so that it's hard to breathe. Laughter is good for the body. It releases endorphins that help you feel good overall and helps clear the mind.

Go read the comics.

Go online and watch a video (I dare you to stop at just one) or more of a dog trying to run up a slide or a cat that misses its landing

Join a laughing club, or start one in your local area.

Recall the last time you had a good belly laugh and chuckle at the silliness of the situation.

That's it. Laugh now, and laugh often.

Stress will come and go, but know that this shift that you're committing to, of engaging in effective stress management, is entirely possible. It may take practice, but it will happen with your dedication. Go now and laugh, be happy, and live in gratitude.

WHAT'S NEXT?

Now that you have gone through this journey towards releasing stress, you might be wondering what is next for you.

Well, if you would like a guide to see how working with crystals can assist you in meditation in particular, I invite you to check out my book, *Your Crystal Journey*:

http://www.amazon.com/dp/B01DJDN54W

Well, you can learn what messages the crystals have specifically for you. Similar to a tarot reading, crystals can be used to give messages relevant to a particular question or situation in mind. I welcome the honor and opportunity of helping you at the following link:

http://www.fiverr.com/mavaldellon

You can also connect with me directly on my site. I often post questions and exercises that challenge you to integrate mind, body, and spirit there, as well as offer a variety of services to energetically assist you. See for yourself what is available:

http://melissavaldellon.com/

Lastly, I want to express my sincerest thanks to you for taking your time to read through this entire guide. I hope you enjoyed these exercises and found them useful towards your healing.

If you found this book helpful and liked it, I would greatly appreciate it if you took a moment to leave a review on Amazon and share this guide with others via social media:

http://www.amazon.com/dp/B00UGIBAIM

ABOUT THE AUTHOR

MELISSA VALDELLON has made it her mission in this lifetime to light your inner flame and inspire you to share and spread that light far and wide.

Melissa has spent this and many lifetimes as a teacher, traditional/native practitioner, healer, priest/priestess, warrior, protector, and more. She draws from a rich depth of experience as she continues to re-awaken to divine knowledge, with the help of her angelic and spiritual team. She knows what it's like to spend years suppressing and denying her given gifts and talents, and ever since she emerged from the spiritual closet, she is passionate about helping others to do the same.

While she currently spends much of her time as an optometrist seeing patients and teaching at the UC Berkeley School of Optometry, she also dedicates much of her time to self-care by meditating, reading, listening to music, spending time with her furry loved ones, visiting the beach, and writing. With two books already published and at least three more on the way, Melissa is certainly keeping busy, but not too busy as to be unavailable to you. You can contact her on her website, and she will personally get back to you shortly.

www.ingramcontent.com/pod-product-compliance
Lightning Source LLC
Chambersburg PA
CBHW061348040426
42444CB00011B/3146